THE GREATEST SALESMAN IN THE WORLD

THE
GREATEST
SALESMAN
IN THE
WORLD

OG MANDINO

BANTAM BOOKS
TORONTO • NEW YORK • LONDON • SYDNEY • AUCKLAND

THE GREATEST SALESMAN IN THE WORLD
*A Bantam Book / published by arrangement with
Frederick Fell, Inc.*

PRINTING HISTORY
*Frederick Fell edition published January 1968
35 printings through 1973
Bantam edition / March 1974
37 printings through January 1983
Bantam Trade edition / February 1985*

Book design by Nicola Mazzella

ISBN 0-553-34156-1

Published simultaneously in the United States and Canada

---

*Bantam Books are published by Bantam Books, Inc. Its trademark,
consisting of the words "Bantam Books" and the portrayal of a
rooster, is Registered in U.S. Patent and Trademark Office and in
other countries. Marca Registrada. Bantam Books, Inc., 666 Fifth
Avenue, New York, New York 10103.*

PRINTED IN THE UNITED STATES OF AMERICA

AH   0 9 8 7 6 5 4 3 2 1

APPRECIATIONS

"The Greatest Salesman in the World is one of the most inspiring, uplifting, and motivating books I have ever read. I can well understand why it has had such a splendid acceptance."

Norman Vincent Peale

"At last! A book on sales and salesmanship that can be read and enjoyed by veteran and recruit alike! I have just completed *The Greatest Salesman in the World* for the second time—it was too good for just one reading—and in all sincerity, I say that it is the most readable, most constructive and most useful instrument for the *teaching* of sales as a profession that I have ever read."

F.W. Errigo, Manager
U.S. Sales Training
Parke, Davis & Company

"I have read almost every book that has ever been written on salesmanship, but I think Og Mandino has captured all of them in *The Greatest Salesman in the World*. No one who follows these principles will ever fail as a salesman, and no one will ever be truly great without them; but, the author has done more than present the principles—he has woven them into the fabric of one of the most fascinating stories I have ever read."

Paul J. Meyer, President
Success Motivation Institute, Inc.

"Every sales manager should read *The Greatest Salesman in the World*. It is a book to keep at the bedside, or on the living room table—a book to dip into as needed, to browse in now and then, to enjoy in small stimulating portions. It is a book for the hour and for the years, a book to turn to over and over again, as to a friend, a book of moral, spiritual and ethical guidance, an unfailing source of comfort and inspiration."

Lester J. Bradshaw, Jr.
Former Dean, Dale Carnegie Institute
of Effective Speaking & Human Relations

"I was overwhelmed by *The Greatest Salesman in the World*. It is, without doubt, the greatest and the most touching story I have ever read. It is so good that there are two musts that I would attach to it: First, you must not lay it down until you have finished it; and secondly, every individual who sells anything, and that includes us all, must read it."

Robert B. Hensley
President, Life Insurance Co.
of Kentucky

"In my opinion, *The Greatest Salesman in the World* by Og Mandino will become a classic. I have published hundreds of books over the years but Og Mandino's powerful message found a place in my innermost being. I am proud to be the publisher of this book."

Frederick V. Fell

CHAPTER ONE

Hafid lingered before the bronze mirror and studied his reflected image in the polished metal.

"Only the eyes have retained their youth," he murmured as he turned away and moved slowly across the spacious marble floor. He passed between black onyx columns rising to support ceilings burnished with silver and gold and his aging legs carried him past tables carved from cyprus and ivory.

Tortoise shell gleamed from couches and divans and the walls, inlaid with gems, shimmered with brocades of the most painstaking design. Huge palms grew placidly in bronze vessels framing a fountain of alabaster nymphs while flower boxes, encrusted with gems, competed with their contents for attention.

No visitor to Hafid's palace could doubt that he was, indeed, a person of great wealth.

The old man passed through an enclosed garden and entered his warehouse which extended beyond the mansion for five hundred paces. Erasmus, his chief bookkeeper, waited uncertainly just beyond the entryway.

"Greetings, sire."

Hafid nodded and continued on in silence. Erasmus followed, his face unable to disguise concern at the master's unusual request for a meeting in this place. Near the loading platforms Hafid paused to watch goods being removed from baggage wagons and counted into separate stalls.

There were wools, fine linens, parchment, honey, carpets, and oil from Asia Minor; glass, figs, nuts, and balsam from his own country; textiles and drugs from Palmyra; ginger, cinnamon, and precious stones from Arabia; corn, paper, granite, alabaster, and basalt from Egypt; tapestries from Babylon; paintings from Rome; and statues from Greece. The smell of balsam was heavy in the air and Hafid's sensitive old nose detected the presence of sweet plums, apples, cheese, and ginger.

Finally he turned to Erasmus. "Old friend, how much wealth is there now accumulated in our treasury?"

Erasmus paled, "Everything, master?"

"Everything."

"I have not studied the numbers recently but I would estimate there is in excess of seven million gold talents."

"And were all the goods in all my warehouses and emporiums converted into gold, how much would they bring?"

"Our inventory is not yet complete for this season, sire, but I would calculate a minimum of another three million talents."

Hafid nodded, "Purchase no more goods. Institute immediately whatever plans are required to sell everything that is mine and convert all of it to gold."

The bookkeeper's mouth opened but no sound came forth. He fell back as if struck and when finally he could speak, the words came with effort.

"I do not understand, sire. This has been our most profitable year. Every emporium reports an increase in sales over the previous season. Even the Roman legions are now our customers for did you not sell the Procurator in Jerusalem two hundred Arabian stallions within the fortnight? Forgive my boldness for seldom have I questioned your orders but this command I cannot comprehend. . . ."

Hafid smiled and gently grasped Erasmus' hand.

"My trusted comrade, is your memory of sufficient strength to recall the first command you received from me when you entered my employ many years ago?"

Erasmus frowned momentarily and then his face brightened. "I was enjoined by you to remove, each year, half the profit from our treasury and dispense it to the poor."

"Did you not, at that time, consider me a foolish man of business?"

"I had great forebodings, sire."

Hafid nodded and spread his arms toward the loading platforms. "Will you now admit that your concern was without ground?"

"Yes, sire."

"Then let me encourage you to maintain faith in this decision until I explain my plans. I am now an old man and my needs are simple. Since my beloved Lisha has been taken from me, after so many years of happiness, it is my desire to distribute all of my wealth among the poor of this city. I shall keep only enough to complete my life without discomfort. Besides disposing of our inventory, I wish you to prepare the necessary documents which will transfer the ownership of every emporium to he who now manages each for me. I also wish you to distribute five thousand gold talents to these managers as a reward for their years of loyalty and so that they may restock their shelves in any manner that they desire."

Erasmus began to speak but Hafid's raised hand silenced him. "Does this assignment seem unpleasant to you?"

The bookkeeper shook his head and attempted to smile. "No, sire, it is only that I cannot understand your reasoning. Your words are those of a man whose days are numbered."

"It is your character, Erasmus, that your concern should be for me instead of yourself. Have ye no thoughts for your own future when our trade empire is disbanded?"

"We have been comrades together for many years. How can I, now, think only of myself?"

Hafid embraced his old friend and replied, "It is not necessary. I ask that you immediately transfer fifty thousand gold talents to your name and I beg that you remain with me until a promise I made long ago is fulfilled. When that promise is kept I will then bequeath this palace and warehouse to you for I will then be ready to rejoin Lisha."

The old bookkeeper stared at his master unable to comprehend the words heard. "Fifty thousand gold talents, the palace, the warehouse . . . I am not deserving. . . . "

Hafid nodded. "I have always counted your friendship as my greatest asset. What I now bestow on you is of little measure compared to your unending loyalty. You have mastered the art of living not for yourself alone, but for others, and this concern has stamped thee above all, as a man among men. Now I urge you to hasten with the consummation of my plans. Time is the most precious commodity I possess and the hour glass of my life is nearly filled."

Erasmus turned his face to hide his tears. His voice broke as he asked, "And what of your promise, yet to keep? Although we have been as brothers never have I heard you talk of such a matter."

Hafid folded his arms and smiled. "I will meet with you again when you have discharged my commands of this morning. Then I will disclose a secret which I have shared with no one, except my beloved wife, for over thirty years."

Chapter
Two

And so it came to pass that a heavily guarded caravan soon departed from Damascus carrying certificates of ownership and gold for those who managed each of Hafid's trade emporiums. From Obed in Joppa to Reuel at Petra, each of the ten managers received word of Hafid's retirement and gift in stunned silence. Eventually, after making its last stop at the emporium in Antipatris, the caravan's mission was complete.

The most powerful trade empire of its time was no more.

His heart heavy with sadness, Erasmus sent word to his master that the warehouse was now empty and the emporiums no longer bore the proud banner of Hafid. The messenger returned with a request that Erasmus meet with his master by the fountain in the peristyle, immediately.

Hafid studied his friend's face and asked, "Is it done?"

"It is done."

"Grieve not, kind friend, and follow me."

Only the sound of their sandals echoed in the giant chamber as Hafid led Erasmus toward the marble stairway at the rear. His steps momentarily slowed as he neared a solitary murrhine vase on a tall stand of citrus wood and he watched as the sunlight changed the glass from white to purple. His old face smiled.

Then the two old friends began to climb the inner steps that led to the room inside the palace dome. Erasmus took notice that the armed guard, always present at the foot of the steps, no longer was there. Finally they reached a landing and paused since both were without breath from the exertion of the climb. Then they continued on to a second landing and Hafid removed a small key from his belt. He unlocked the heavy oak door and leaned against it until it creaked inwards. Erasmus hesitated until his master beckoned him inside and then he stepped timidly into the room to which no one had been allowed admission for over three decades.

Grey and dusty light seeped down from turrets above and Erasmus gripped Hafid's arm until his eyes became accustomed to the semi-darkness. With a faint smile, Hafid watched as Erasmus turned slowly in a room that was bare except for a small cedar chest spotlighted in a shaft of sunlight in one corner.

"Are you not disappointed, Erasmus?"

"I know not what to say, sire."

"Are you not disappointed in the furnishings? Certainly the contents of this room have been a conversation piece among many. Have you not wondered or concerned yourself with the mystery of what is contained here which I have guarded so zealously for so long?"

Erasmus nodded, "It is true. There has been much talk and many rumors through the years as to what our master kept hidden here in the tower."

"Yes, my friend, and most of them I have heard. It has been said that barrels of diamonds were here, and gold ingots, or wild animals, or rare birds. Once a Persian rug merchant hinted that perhaps I maintained a small harem here. Lisha laughed at the thought of me with a collection of concubines. But, as you can observe, there is nothing here except a small chest. Now, come forward."

The two men crouched beside the chest and Hafid carefully proceeded to unroll the leather strapping which encircled it. He inhaled deeply of the cedar fragrance from the wood and finally he pushed against the cover and it quietly sprung open. Erasmus leaned forward and stared over Hafid's shoulder at the trunk's contents. He looked at Hafid and shook his head in bewilderment. There was nothing inside the trunk but scrolls . . . leather scrolls.

Hafid reached inside and gently removed one of the rolls. Momentarily he clasped it to his breast and closed his eyes. A quiet calmness settled over his face, brushing away the lines of age. Then he rose to his feet and pointed toward the chest.

"Were this room filled to its beams with diamonds, its value could not surpass what your eyes behold in this simple wooden box. All the success, happiness, love, peace of mind, and wealth that I have enjoyed is directly traceable to what is contained in these few scrolls. My debt to them and to the wise one who entrusted them to my care can never be repaid."

Frightened by the tone in Hafid's voice, Erasmus stepped back and asked, "Is this the secret to which you have referred? Is this chest connected in some way with the promise you have yet to keep?"

"The answer is 'yes' to both of your questions."

Erasmus passed his hand across his perspiring forehead and looked at Hafid with disbelief. "What is written on these scrolls that places their value beyond that of diamonds?"

"All but one of these scrolls contain a principle, a law, or a fundamental truth written in a unique style to help the reader understand its meaning. To become a master in the art of sales one must learn and practice the secret of each scroll. When one masters these principles one has the power to accumulate all the wealth he desires."

Erasmus stared at the old scrolls with dismay. "As wealthy even, as you?"

"Far wealthier, if he chooses."

"You have stated that all but one of these scrolls contain selling principles. What is contained on the last scroll?"

"The last scroll, as you call it, is the first scroll which must be read, since each is numbered to be read in a special sequence. And the first scroll contains a secret which has been given to a mere handful of wise men throughout history. The first scroll, in truth, teaches the most effective way to learn what is written on the others."

"It seems to be a task that anyone can master."

"It is, indeed, a simple task provided one is willing to pay the price in time and concentration until each principle becomes a part of one's personality; until each principle becomes a habit in living."

Erasmus reached into the chest and removed a scroll. Holding it gently between his fingers and his thumb, he shook it toward Hafid. "Forgive me, master, but why is it that you have not shared these principles with others, especially those who have labored long in your employ? You have always shown such generosity in all other matters, how is it that all who have sold for you did not receive the opportunity to read these words of wisdom and thus become wealthy too? At the very least, all would have been better sellers of goods with such valuable knowledge. Why have you kept these principles to yourself for all these years?"

"I had no choice. Many years ago when these scrolls were entrusted to my care, I was made to promise under oath, that I would share their contents with only one person. I do not yet understand the reasoning behind this strange request. However, I was commanded to apply the principles of the scrolls to my own life, until one day someone would appear who had need for the help and guidance contained in these scrolls far more than I did when I was a youth. I was told that through some sign I would recognize the individual to whom I was to pass the scrolls even though it was possible that the individual would not know that he was seeking the scrolls.

"I have waited patiently, and while I waited I applied these principles as I was given permission to do. With their knowledge I became what many call the greatest salesman in the world just as he who bequeathed these scrolls to me was acclaimed as the greatest salesman of his time. Now, Erasmus, perhaps you will understand, at last, why some of my actions through the years seemed peculiar and unworkable to you, yet they proved successful. Always were my deeds and decisions guided by these scrolls; therefore, it was not through my wisdom that we acquired so many gold talents. I was only the instrument of fulfillment."

"Do you still believe that he who is to receive these scrolls from thee will appear after all this time?"

"Yes."

Hafid gently replaced the scrolls and closed the chest. He spoke softly from his knees, "Will you stay with me until that day, Erasmus?"

The bookkeeper reached through soft light until their hands clasped. He nodded once and then withdrew from the room as if from an unspoken command from his master. Hafid replaced the leather strapping on the chest and then stood and walked to a small turret. He stepped through it out onto the scaffold that surrounded the great dome.

A wind from the East blew into the old man's face carrying with it the smell of the lakes and the desert beyond. He smiled as he stood high above the rooftops of Damascus and his thoughts leaped backwards through time. . . .

CHAPTER THREE

It was winter and the chill was bitter on the Mount of Olives. From Jerusalem, across the narrow cleft of the Kidron Valley, came the smell of smoke, incense, and burning flesh from the Temple and its foulness mixed with the turpentine odor of terebinth trees on the mountain.

On an open slope, only a short descent from the village of Bethpage, slumbered the immense trade caravan of Pathros of Palmyra. The hour was late and even the great merchant's favorite stallion had ceased munching on the low pistachio bushes and settled down against a soft hedge of laurel.

Beyond the long row of silent tents, strands of thick hemp curled around four ancient olive trees. They formed a square corral enclosing shapeless forms of camels and asses huddled together to draw warmth from each other's body. Except for two guards, patrolling near the baggage wagons, the only movement in the camp was the tall and moving shadow outlined against the goat's hair wall of Pathros' great tent.

Inside, Pathros paced angrily back and forth, pausing occasionally to frown and shake his head at the youth kneeling timidly near the tent opening. Finally he lowered his ailing body to the gold-woven rug and beckoned the lad to move closer.

"Hafid, you have always been as my own. I am perplexed and puzzled by your strange request. Are you not content with your work?"

The boy's eyes were fixed on the rug. "No, sire."

"Perhaps the ever increasing size of our caravans has made your task of tending to all our animals too great?"

"No, sire."

"Then kindly repeat your request. Include also, in thy words, the reasoning behind such an unusual request."

"It is my desire to become a seller of your goods instead of only your camel boy. I wish to become as Hadad, Simon, Caleb, and the others who depart from our baggage wagons with animals barely able to crawl from the weight of your goods and who return with gold for thee and gold also for themselves. I desire to improve my lowly position in life. As a camel boy I am nothing, but as a salesman for you I can acquire wealth and success."

"How do you know this?"

"Often have I heard you say that no other trade

or profession has more opportunity for one to rise from poverty to great wealth than that of salesman."

Pathros began to nod but thought better of it and continued to question the youth. "Dost thou believe you are capable of performing as Hadad and the other sellers?"

Hafid stared intently at the old man and replied, "Many times have I overheard Caleb complain to you about misfortunes that accounted for his lack of sales and many times have I heard you remind him that anyone could sell all the goods in your warehouse within a small passing of time if he but applied himself to learn the principles and laws of selling. If you believe that Caleb, whom everyone calls a fool, can learn these principles, then cannot I also acquire this special knowledge?"

"If you should master these principles what would be your goal in life?"

Hafid hesitated and then said, "It has been repeated throughout the land that you are a great salesman. The world has never seen a trade empire such as you have built through your mastery of salesmanship. My ambition is to become even greater than you, the greatest merchant, the wealthiest man, and the greatest salesman in all the world!"

Pathros leaned back and studied the young, dark face. The smell from the animals was still on his clothes but the youth displayed little humility in his manner. "And what will you do with all this great wealth and the fearsome power that will surely accompany it?"

"I will do as you do. My family will be provided with the finest of worldly goods and the rest I will share with those in need."

Pathros shook his head. "Wealth, my son, should never be your goal in life. Your words are eloquent but they are mere words. True wealth is of the heart, not of the purse."

Hafid persisted, "Art thou not wealthy, sire?"

The old man smiled at Hafid's boldness. "Hafid, so far as material wealth is concerned, there is only one difference between myself and the lowliest beggar outside Herod's palace. The beggar thinks only of his next meal and I think only of the meal that will be my last. No, my son, do not aspire for wealth and labor not only to be rich. Strive instead for happiness, to be loved and to love, and most important, to acquire peace of mind and serenity."

Hafid continued to persist. "But these things are impossible without gold. Who can live in poverty with peace of mind? How can one be happy with an empty stomach? How can one demonstrate love for one's family if he is unable to feed and clothe and house them? You, yourself, have said that wealth is good when it brings joy to others. Why then is my ambition to be wealthy not a good one? Poverty may be a privilege and even a way of life for the monk in the desert, for he has only himself to sustain and none but his god to please, but I consider poverty to be the mark of a lack of ability or a lack of ambition. I am not deficient in either of these qualities!"

Pathros frowned, "What has caused this sudden outburst of ambition? You speak of providing for a family yet you have no family lest it be I who have adopted you since the pestilence removed thy mother and father."

Hafid's sun-darkened skin could not hide the sudden flush in his cheeks. "While we encamped in Hebron before journeying here I met the daughter of Calneh. She . . . she . . ."

"Oh, ho, now the truth emergeth. Love, not noble ideals, has changed my camel boy into a mighty soldier ready to battle the world. Calneh is a very wealthy man. His daughter and a camel boy? Never! But his daughter and a rich, young, and handsome merchant . . . ah, that is another matter. Very well, my young soldier, I will help you begin your career as a salesman."

The lad fell to his knees and grasped Pathros' robe. "Sire, sire! How can I say the words to show my thanks?"

Pathros freed himself from Hafid's grip and stepped back. "I would suggest you withhold thy thanks for the present. Whatever aid I give thee will be as a grain of sand compared to the mountains you must move for yourself."

Hafid's joy immediately subsided as he asked, "Will you not teach me the principles and laws that will transform me into a great salesman?"

"I will not. No more than I have made your early youth soft and easy through pampering. I have been criticized often for condemning my adopted son to the life of a camel boy but I believed that if the right fire was burning inside it would eventually emerge . . . and when it did you would be far more a man for your years of difficult toil. Tonight, your request has made me happy for the fire of ambition glows in your eyes and your face shines with burning desire. This is good and my judgment is vindicated but you must still prove that there is more behind your words than air."

Hafid was silent and the old man continued, "First, you must prove to me, and more important to yourself, that you can endure the life of a salesman for it is not an easy lot you have chosen. Truly, many times have you heard me say that the rewards are great if one succeeds but the rewards are great only because so few succeed. Many succumb to despair and fail without realizing that they already possess all the tools needed to acquire great wealth. Many others face each obstacle in their path with fear and doubt and consider them as enemies when, in truth, these obstructions are friends and helpers. Obstacles are necessary for success because in selling, as in all careers of importance, victory comes only after many struggles and countless defeats. Yet each struggle, each defeat, sharpens your skills and strengths, your courage and your endurance, your ability and your confidence and thus each obstacle is a comrade-in-arms forcing you to become better . . . or quit. Each rebuff is an opportunity to move forward; turn away from them, avoid them, and you throw away your future."

The youth nodded and made as if to speak but the old man raised his hand and continued, "Furthermore, you are embarking on the loneliest profession in the world. Even the despised tax collectors return to their homes at sundown and the legions of

Rome have a barracks to call home. But you will witness many setting suns far from all friends and loved ones. Nothing can bring the hurt of loneliness upon a man so swiftly as to pass a strange house in the dark and witness, in the lamplight from within, a family breaking evening bread together.

"It is in these periods of loneliness that temptations will confront thee," Pathros continued. "How you meet these temptations will greatly affect your career. When you are on the road with only your animal it is a strange and often frightening sensation. Often our perspectives and our values are temporarily forgotten and we become like children, longing for the safety and love of our own. What we find as a substitute has ended the career of many including thousands who were considered to have great potential in the art of selling. Furthermore, there will be no one to humor you or console you when you have sold no goods; no one except those who seek to separate you from your money pouch."

"I will be careful and heed thy words of warning."

"Then let us begin. For the present you will receive no more advice. You stand before me as a green fig. Until the fig is ripe it cannot be called a fig and until you have been exposed to knowledge and experience you cannot be called a salesman."

"How shall I begin?"

"In the morning you are to report to Silvio at the baggage wagons. He will release, in your charge, one of our finest seamless robes. It is woven from the hair of a goat and will withstand even the heaviest rains and it is dyed red from the roots of the madder plant so that the color will always hold fast. Near the hem you will find sewn on the inside, a small star. This is the mark of Tola whose guild makes the finest robes in all the world. Next to the star is my mark, a circle within a square. Both these marks are known and respected throughout the land and we have sold countless thousands of these robes. I have dealt with the Jews so long that I only know their name for such a garment as this. It is called an *abeyah*.

"Take the robe and a donkey and depart at dawn for Bethlehem, the village which our caravan passed through before arriving here. None of our sellers ever visit there. They report that it is a waste of their time because the people are so poor, yet many years ago I sold hundreds of robes among the shepherds there. Remain in Bethlehem until you have sold the robe."

Hafid nodded, attempting in vain to conceal his excitement. "At what price shall I sell the robe, master?"

"I will enter a charge of one silver denarius against your name on my ledger. When you return you will remit one silver denarius to me. Keep all that you receive in excess of this as your commission, so, in fact, you set the price of the robe yourself. You may visit the market place which is at the south entry of town or you may wish to consider calling on each dwelling in the town itself, of which I am certain there are over a thousand. Certainly it is conceivable that one robe can be sold there, do you not agree?"

Hafid nodded again, his mind already on the morrow.

Pathros placed his hand gently on the lad's shoulder. "I will place no one in your position until you return. If you discover that your stomach is not for this profession I will understand and you must not consider yourself in disgrace. Never feel shame for trying and failing for he who has never failed is he who has never tried. Upon your return I will question you at length concerning your experiences. Then I will decide how I shall proceed with helping you to make your outlandish dreams come true."

Hafid bowed and turned to leave but the old man was not finished. "Son, there is one precept that you must remember as you begin this new life. Keep it always in your mind and you will overcome seemingly impossible obstacles that are certain to confront you as they do everyone with ambition."

Hafid waited. "Yes, sire?"

"Failure will never overtake you if your determination to succeed is strong enough."

Pathros stepped close to the youth. "Do you comprehend the full meaning of my words?"

"Yes, sire."

"Then repeat them to me!"

"*Failure will never overtake me if my determination to succeed is strong enough.*"

CHAPTER FOUR

Hafid pushed aside the half-eaten loaf of bread and considered his unhappy fate. Tomorrow would be his fourth day in Bethlehem and the single red robe that he had carried so confidently away from the caravan was still in the pack on the back of his animal, now tethered to a stake in the cave behind the inn.

He heard not the noise that surrounded him in the overcrowded dining hall as he scowled at his unfinished meal. Doubts that have assailed every seller since the beginning of time passed through his mind:

"Why will the people not listen to my story? How does one command their attention? Why do they close their door before I have said five words? Why do they lose interest in my talk and walk away?

Is everyone poor in this town? What can I say when they tell me they like the robe but cannot afford it? Why do so many tell me to return at a later date? How do others sell when I cannot? What is this fear that seizes me when I approach a closed door and how can I overcome it? Is my price not in line with the other sellers?"

He shook his head in disgust at his failure. Perhaps this was not the life for him. Perhaps he should remain a camel boy and continue earning only coppers for each day's labor. As a seller of goods he would indeed be fortunate if he returned to the caravan with any profit at all. What had Pathros called him? A young soldier? He wished, momentarily, that he were back with his animals.

Then his thoughts turned to Lisha and to her stern father, Calneh, and the doubts quickly left his mind. Tonight he would again sleep in the hills to conserve his funds and tomorrow he would sell the robe. Furthermore, he would speak with such eloquence that the robe would bring a good price. He would begin early, just after dawn, and station himself near the town well. He would address everyone that approached and within a short time he would be returning to the Mount of Olives with silver in his purse.

He reached for the unfinished bread and began to eat while he thought of his master. Pathros would be proud of him because he had not despaired and returned as a failure. In truth, four days was much too long a time to consummate the sale of but one simple robe but if he could accomplish the deed in four days he knew he could learn, from Pathros, how to accomplish it in three days, then two days. In time he would become so proficient that he would sell many robes every hour! Then he would indeed be a salesman of repute.

He departed from the noisy inn and headed toward the cave and his animal. The chilled air had stiffened the grass with a thin coating of frost and each blade crackled with complaint from the pressure of his sandals. Hafid decided not to ride into the hills tonight. Instead, he would rest in the cave with his animal.

Tomorrow, he knew, would be a better day although now he understood why the others always bypassed this unprosperous village. They had said that no sales could be made here and he had recalled their words every time someone had refused to buy his robe. Yet, Pathros had sold hundreds of robes here many years ago. Perhaps times had been different then and, after all, Pathros was a great salesman.

A flickering light from the cave caused him to hasten his steps for fear that a thief was within. He rushed through the opening in the limestone ready to overcome the criminal and recover his possessions. Instead, the tenseness immediately left his body at the sight that confronted him.

A small candle, forced between a cleft in the cave wall, shone faintly on a bearded man and a young woman huddled closely together. At their feet, in a hollowed-out stone that usually held cattle fodder, slept an infant. Hafid knew little of such things but he sensed that the baby was newborn from the child's wrinkled and crimson skin. To protect the sleeping infant from the cold, both the man's and the woman's cloaks covered all but the small head.

The man nodded in Hafid's direction while the woman moved closer to the child. No one spoke. Then the woman trembled and Hafid saw that her thin garment offered little protection against the dampness of the cave. Hafid looked again at the infant. He watched, fascinated, as the small mouth opened and closed, almost in a smile, and a strange sensation passed through him. For some unknown reason he thought of Lisha. The woman trembled again from the cold and her sudden movement returned Hafid from his daydreaming.

After painful moments of indecision the would-be seller of goods walked to his animal. He carefully untied the knots, opened his pack, and withdrew the robe. He unrolled it and rubbed his hands over the material. The red dye glowed in the candlelight and he could see the mark of Pathros and the mark of Tola on its underside. The circle in the square and the star. How many times had he held this robe in his tired arms in the past three days? It seemed as if he knew every weave and fiber of it. This was indeed a robe of quality. With care it would last a lifetime.

Hafid closed his eyes and sighed. Then he walked swiftly toward the small family, knelt on the straw beside the infant, and gently removed first the father's tattered cloak and then the mother's from the manger. He handed each back to its owner. Both were too shocked at Hafid's boldness to react. Then Hafid opened his precious red robe and wrapped it gently around the sleeping child.

Moisture from the young mother's kiss was still on Hafid's cheek as he led his animal out of the cave. Directly above him was the brightest star Hafid had ever seen. He stared up at it until his eyes filled with tears and then he headed his animal through the path that led toward the main road back to Jerusalem and the caravan on the mountain.

CHAPTER
FIVE

Hafid rode slowly, his head bowed so that he no longer noticed the star spreading its path of light before him. Why had he committed such a foolish act? He knew not those people in the cave. Why had he not attempted to sell the robe to them? What would he tell Pathros? And the others? They would roll on the ground with laughter when they learned he had given away a robe with which he had been charged. And to a strange baby in a cave. He searched his mind for a tale that would deceive Pathros. Perhaps he could say that the robe had been stolen from his animal while he was in the dining hall. Would Pathros believe such a tale? After all, there were many bandits in the land. And should Pathros believe him would he not then be condemned for carelessness?

All too soon he reached the path that led through the Garden of Gethsemane. He dismounted and walked wearily ahead of the mule until he arrived at the caravan. The light from above made it seem as daylight and the confrontation he had been dreading was quickly upon him as he saw Pathros, outside his tent, staring into the heavens. Hafid remained motionless but the old man noticed him almost immediately.

There was awe in the voice of Pathros as he approached the youth and asked, "Have you come directly from Bethlehem?"

"Yes, master."

"Are you not alarmed that a star should follow you?"

"I had not noticed, sire."

"Had not noticed? I have been unable to move from this spot since I first saw that star rise over Bethlehem nearly two hours ago. Never have I seen one with more color and brightness. Then as I watched, it began to move in the heavens and approach our caravan. Now that it is directly overhead, you appear, and by the gods, it moves no more."

Pathros approached Hafid and studied the youth's face closely as he asked, "Did you participate in some extraordinary event while in Bethlehem?"

"No, sire."

The old man frowned as if deep in thought. "I have never known a night or an experience such as this."

Hafid flinched. "This night I shall never forget either, master."

"Oh, ho, then something did indeed happen this evening. How is it that thou returneth at such a late hour?"

Hafid was silent as the old man turned and prodded at the pack on Hafid's mule. "It is empty! Success at last. Come into my tent and tell me of your experiences. Since the gods have turned night into day I cannot sleep and perhaps your words will furnish some clue as to why a star should follow a camel boy."

Pathros reclined on his cot and listened with closed eyes to Hafid's long tale of endless refusals, rebuffs, and insults which had been encountered in Bethlehem. Occasionally he would nod as when Hafid described the pottery merchant who had thrown him bodily from his shop and he smiled when told of the Roman soldier who had flung the robe back in Hafid's face when the young seller had refused to reduce his price.

Finally Hafid, his voice hoarse and muffled, was describing all the doubts that had beset him in the inn this very evening. Pathros interrupted him, "Hafid, as well as you can recall, relate to me every doubt that passed through your mind as you sat feeling sorry for yourself."

When Hafid had named them all to the best of his recollection, the old man asked, "Now, what thought finally entered your mind which drove away the doubts and gave you new courage to decide to try again to sell the robe on the morrow?"

Hafid considered his reply for a moment and then said, "I thought only of the daughter of Calneh.

Even in that foul inn I knew that I could never face her again if I failed." Then Hafid's voice broke, "But I failed her, anyway."

"You failed? I do not understand. The robe did not return with thee."

In a voice so low that Pathros found it necessary to lean forward in order to hear, Hafid related the incident of the cave, the infant, and the robe. As the youth spoke, Pathros glanced again and again at the open tent flap and the brightness beyond which still illuminated the camp grounds. A smile began to form on his puzzled face and he did not notice that the lad had ceased with his story and was now sobbing.

Soon the sobs subsided and there was only silence in the great tent. Hafid dared not look up at his master. He had failed and proven that he was ill-equipped to be anything more than a camel boy. He fought back the urge to leap up and run from the tent. Then he felt the great salesman's hand on his shoulder and forced himself to look into the eyes of Pathros.

"My son, this trip has not been of much profit to you."

"No, sire."

"But to me it has. The star which followed you has cured me of a blindness that I am reluctant to admit. I will explain this matter to you only after we return to Palmyra. Now I make a request of thee."

"Yes, master."

"Our sellers will begin returning to the caravan before sundown tomorrow and their animals will need your care. Are you willing to return to your duties as camel boy for the present?"

Hafid rose resignedly and bowed toward his benefactor. "Whatever you ask of me, that I will do . . . and I am sorry that I have failed you."

"Go then, and prepare for the return of our men and we shall meet again when we are in Palmyra."

As Hafid stepped through the tent opening, bright light from above momentarily blinded him. He rubbed his eyes and heard Pathros call from inside the tent.

The youth turned and stepped back inside, waiting for the old man to speak. Pathros pointed toward him and said, "Sleep in peace for you have not failed."

The bright star remained above throughout the night.

CHAPTER
SIX

Nearly a fortnight after the caravan had returned to its headquarters in Palmyra, Hafid was awakened from his straw cot in the stable, and summoned to appear before Pathros.

He hastened to the bed chamber of the master and stood uncertainly before the huge bed which dwarfed its occupant. Pathros opened his eyes and struggled with his coverings until he was sitting upright. His face was gaunt and blood vessels bulged in his hands. It was difficult for Hafid to believe that this was the same man with whom he had spoken only twelve days ago.

Pathros motioned toward the lower half of the bed and the youth sat carefully on its edge, waiting for the old man to speak. Even Pathros' voice was different in sound and pitch from their last meeting.

"My son, ye have had many days to reconsider your ambitions. Is it still within thee to become a great salesman?"

"Yes, sire."

The ancient head nodded. "So be it. I had planned to spend much time with you but as you can see there are other plans for me. Although I consider myself a good salesman I am unable to sell death on departing from my door. He has been waiting for days like a hungry dog at our kitchen door. Like the dog, he knows that eventually the door will be left unguarded. . . ."

Coughing interrupted Pathros and Hafid sat motionless as the old man gasped for air. Finally the coughs ceased and Pathros smiled weakly, "Our time together is brief so let us begin. First, remove the small cedar chest which is beneath this bed."

Hafid knelt and pulled out a small leather-strapped box. He placed it below the contour made by Pathros' legs on the bed. The old man cleared his throat, "Many years ago when I possessed less status than even a camel boy, I was privileged to rescue a traveler from the East who had been set upon by two bandits. He insisted that I had saved his life and wished to reward me although I sought none. Since I had neither a family nor funds he enjoined me to return with him to his home and kin where I was accepted as one of his own.

"One day, after I had grown accustomed to my new life, he introduced me to this chest. Inside were ten leather scrolls, each one numbered. The first contained the secret of learning. The others contained all the secrets and principles necessary to become a great success in the art of selling. For the next year I was tutored each day on the wise words of the scrolls and with the secret of learning from the first scroll I eventually memorized every word on every scroll until they had become a part of my thinking and my life. They became habit.

"At last I was presented with the chest containing all ten scrolls, a sealed letter, and a purse containing fifty gold pieces. The sealed letter was not to be opened until my adopted home was out of sight. I bade the family farewell and waited until I had reached the trade route to Palmyra before opening the letter. The contents commanded me to take the gold pieces, apply what I had learned from the scrolls, and begin a new life. The letter further commanded me to always share half of whatever wealth I would acquire with others less fortunate, but the leather scrolls were neither to be given nor shared with anyone until the day when I would be given a special sign that would tell me who was next chosen to receive these scrolls."

Hafid shook his head, "I do not understand, sire."

"I will explain. I have remained on watch for this person with a sign for many years and while I watched I applied what I learned from the scrolls to amass a great fortune. I had almost come to believe that no such person would ever appear before my death until you returned from your trip to Bethlehem. My first inkling that you were the chosen one to receive the scrolls came upon me when you appeared under the bright star that had followed you from Bethlehem. In my heart I have tried to comprehend the meaning of this event but I am resigned not to challenge the actions of the gods. Then when you told me of giving up the robe, which meant so much to you, something within my heart spoke and told me that my long search was ended. I had finally found he who was ordained to next receive the chest. Strangely, as soon as I knew I had found the right one, my life's energy began to slowly drain away. Now I am near the end but my long search is over and I can depart from this world in peace."

The old man's voice grew faint but he clenched his bony fists and leaned closer to Hafid. "Listen closely, my son, for I will have no strength to repeat these words."

Hafid's eyes were moist as he moved nearer to his master. Their hands touched and the great salesman inhaled with effort. "I now pass on this chest and its valuable contents to thee but first there are certain conditions to which you must agree. In the chest is a purse with one hundred gold talents. This will enable you to live and purchase a small supply of rugs with which you can enter the business world. I could bestow on you great wealth but this would do you a terrible disservice. Far better is it that you become the world's wealthiest and greatest salesman on your own. You see, I have not forgotten your goal.

"Depart from this city immediately and go to Damascus. There you will find unlimited opportunities to apply what the scrolls will teach. After you have secured lodging you will open only the scroll marked One. You are to read this over and over until you understand fully the secret method which it relates and which you will use in learning the principles of selling success contained on all the other scrolls. As you learn from each scroll you can begin to sell the rugs you have purchased, and if you combine what you learn with the experience you acquire, and continue to study each scroll as instructed, your sales will grow in number each day. My first condition then is that you must swear under oath that you will follow the instructions contained in the scroll marked One. Do you agree?"

"Yes, sire."

"Good, good . . . and when you apply the principles of the scrolls you will become far wealthier than you have ever dreamed. My second condition is that you must constantly dispose of half your earnings to those less fortunate than you. There must be no deviation from this condition. Will you agree?"

"Yes, sire."

"And now the most important condition of all. You are forbidden to share the scrolls or the wisdom they contain with anyone. One day there will appear a person who will transmit to you a sign just as the star and your unselfish actions were the sign I sought. When this happens you will recognize this sign even though the person transmitting it may be ignorant that he is the chosen person. When your heart assures you that you are correct you will pass over to him, or her, the chest and its contents and when this is done there need be no conditions imposed on the receiver such as were imposed on me and which I now impose on you. The letter which I received so long ago commanded that the third to receive the scrolls could share their message with the world if he so desires. Will you promise to carry out this third condition?"

"I will."

Pathros sighed in relief as if a heavy weight had been removed from his body. He smiled weakly and cupped Hafid's face in his bony hands. "Take the chest and depart. I will see thee no more. Go with my love and with my wishes for success and may your Lisha eventually share all the happiness your future will bring you."

Tears unashamedly rolled down Hafid's cheeks as he took the chest and carried it through the open bedroom door. He paused outside, placed the chest on the floor, and turned back toward his master, "Failure will never overtake me if my determination to succeed is strong enough?"

The old man smiled faintly and nodded. He raised his hand in farewell.

CHAPTER SEVEN

Hafid, with his animal, entered the walled city of Damascus through the East gate. He rode along the street called Straight with doubts and trepidations and the noise and shoutings from hundreds of bazaars did little to ease his fear. It was one thing to arrive in a large city with a powerful trade caravan such as that of Pathros; it was another to be unprotected and alone. Street merchants rushed at him from all sides holding up merchandise, each screaming louder than the next. He passed cell-like shops and bazaars displaying craftsmanship of coppersmiths, silversmiths, saddlers, weavers, carpenters; and each step of his mule brought him face to face with another vender, hands outstretched, wailing words of self-pity.

Directly ahead of him, beyond the western wall

of the city, rose Mt. Hermon. Although the season was summer, its top was still capped with white and it seemed to look down on the cacophony of the market place with tolerance and forbearance. Eventually Hafid turned off the famous street and inquired about lodging which he had no difficulty finding in an inn called Moscha. His room was clean and he paid his rent for a month in advance which immediately established his standing with Antonine, the owner. Then he stabled his animal behind the inn, bathed himself in the waters of the Barada and returned to his room.

He placed the small cedar chest at the foot of his cot and proceeded to unroll the leather strappings. The cover opened easily and he gazed down at the leather scrolls. Finally he reached inside and touched the leather. It gave under his fingers as if it were alive and he hurriedly withdrew his hand. He arose and stepped toward the latticed window through which sounds poured from the noisy market place nearly half a mile distant. Fear and doubt returned again as he looked in the direction of the muffled voices and he felt his confidence waning. He closed his eyes, leaned his head against the wall, and cried aloud, "How foolish I am to dream that I, a mere camel boy, will one day be acclaimed as the greatest salesman in the world when I have not even the courage to ride through the stalls of the hawkers in the street. Today mine eyes have witnessed hundreds of salesmen, all far better equipped for their profession than I. All had boldness, enthusiasm, and persistence. All seemed equipped to survive in

the jungle of the market. How stupid and presump-
tuous to think I can compete with and surpass them.
Pathros, my Pathros, I fear that I will fail you again."

He threw himself on his cot and weary from his
travels he sobbed until he slept.

When he awoke it was morning. Even before he
opened his eyes he heard the chirp. Then he sat up
and stared in disbelief at the sparrow perched on the
open cover of the chest containing the scrolls. He
ran to the window. Outside, thousands of sparrows
clustered in the fig trees and sycamores, each wel-
coming the day with song. As he watched, some
landed on the window ledge but quickly flew away
when Hafid moved even slightly. Then he turned
and looked at the chest again. His feathered visitor
cocked its head and stared back at the youth.

Hafid walked slowly to the chest, his hand extended. The bird leaped into his palm. "Thousands
of your kind are outside and afraid. But you had the
courage to come through the window."

The bird pecked sharply at Hafid's skin and the
youth carried him toward the table where his knap-
sack contained bread and cheese. He broke off chunks
and placed them beside his small friend who began
to eat.

A thought came to Hafid and he returned to the
window. He rubbed his hand against the openings
in the lattice. They were so small that it seemed
almost impossible for the sparrow to have entered.
Then he remembered the voice of Pathros and he
repeated the words aloud, "Failure will never over-

take you if your determination to succeed is strong enough."

He returned to the chest and reached inside. One leather scroll was more worn than the rest. He removed it from the box and gently unrolled it. The fear he had known was gone. Then he looked toward the sparrow. He too was gone. Only crumbs of bread and cheese remained as evidence of his visit from the little bird with courage. Hafid glanced down at the scroll. Its heading read *The Scroll Marked I.* He began to read. . . .

CHAPTER EIGHT

The Scroll Marked I

Today I begin a new life.

Today I shed my old skin which hath, too long, suffered the bruises of failure and the wounds of mediocrity.

Today I am born anew and my birthplace is a vineyard where there is fruit for all.

Today I will pluck grapes of wisdom from the tallest and fullest vines in the vineyard, for these were planted by the wisest of my profession who have come before me, generation upon generation.

Today I will savor the taste of grapes from these vines and verily I will swallow the seed of success buried in each and new life will sprout within me.

The career I have chosen is laden with opportunity yet it is fraught with heartbreak and despair and the bodies of those who have failed, were they piled one atop another, would cast its shadow down upon all the pyramids of the earth.

Yet I will not fail, as the others, for in my hands I now hold the charts which will guide me through perilous waters to shores which only yesterday seemed but a dream.

Failure no longer will be my payment for struggle. Just as nature made no provision for my body to tolerate pain neither has it made any provision for my life to suffer failure. Failure, like pain, is alien to my life. In the past I accepted it as I accepted pain. Now I reject it and I am prepared for wisdom and principles which will guide me out of the shadows into the sunlight of wealth, position, and happiness far beyond my most extravagant dreams until even the golden apples in the Garden of Hesperides will seem no more than my just reward.

Time teaches all things to he who lives forever but I have not the luxury of eternity. Yet, within my allotted time I must practice the art of patience for nature acts never in haste. To create the olive, king of all trees, a hundred years is required. An onion plant is old in nine weeks. I have lived as an onion plant. It has not pleased me. Now I wouldst become the greatest of olive trees and, in truth, the greatest of salesmen.

And how will this be accomplished? For I have neither the knowledge nor the experience to achieve greatness and already I have stumbled in ignorance and fallen into pools of self-pity. The answer is simple. I will commence my journey unencumbered with either the weight of unnecessary knowledge or the handicap of meaningless experience. Nature already has supplied me with knowledge and instinct far greater than any beast in the forest and the value of experience is overrated, usually by old men who nod wisely and speak stupidly.

In truth, experience teaches thoroughly yet her course of instruction devours men's years so the value of her lessons diminishes with the time necessary to acquire her special wisdom. The end finds it wasted on dead men. Furthermore, experience is comparable to fashion; an action that proved successful today will be unworkable and impractical tomorrow.

Only principles endure and these I now possess, for the laws that will lead me to greatness are contained in the words of these scrolls. What they will teach me is more to prevent failure than to gain success, for what is success other than a state of mind? Which two, among a thousand wise men, will define success in the same words; yet failure is always described but one way. *Failure is man's inability to reach his goals in life, whatever they may be.*

In truth, the only difference between those who have failed and those who have succeeded lies in the difference of their habits. Good habits are the key to all success. Bad habits are the unlocked door to failure. Thus, the first law I will obey, which precedeth all others is—*I will form good habits and become their slaves.*

As a child I was slave to my impulses; now I am slave to my habits, as are all grown men. I have surrendered my free will to the years of accumulated habits and the past deeds of my life have already marked out a path which threatens to imprison my future. My actions are ruled by appetite, passion, prejudice, greed, love, fear, environment, habit, and the worst of these tyrants is habit. Therefore, if I must be a slave to habit let me be a slave to good habits. My bad habits must be destroyed and new furrows prepared for good seed.

I will form good habits and become their slave.

And how will I accomplish this difficult feat? Through these scrolls, it will be done, for each scroll contains a principle which will drive a bad habit from my life and replace it with one which will bring me closer to success. For it is another of nature's laws that only a habit can subdue another habit. So, in order for these written words to perform their chosen task, I must discipline myself with the first of my new habits which is as follows:

I will read each scroll for thirty days in this prescribed manner, before I proceed to the next scroll.

First, I will read the words in silence when I arise. Then, I will read the words in silence after I have partaken of my midday meal. Last, I will read the words again just before I retire at day's end, and most important, on this occasion I will read the words aloud.

On the next day I will repeat this procedure, and I will continue in like manner for thirty days. Then, I will turn to the next scroll and repeat this procedure for another thirty days. I will continue in this manner until I have lived with each scroll for thirty days and my reading has become habit.

And what will be accomplished with this habit? Herein lies the hidden secret of all man's accomplishments. As I repeat the words daily they will soon become a part of my active mind, but more important, they will also seep into my other mind, that mysterious source which never sleeps, which creates my dreams, and often makes me act in ways I do not comprehend.

As the words of these scrolls are consumed by my mysterious mind I will begin to awake, each morning, with a vitality I have never known before. My vigor will increase, my enthusiasm will rise, my desire to meet the world will overcome every fear I once knew at sunrise, and I will be happier than I ever believed it possible to be in this world of strife and sorrow.

Eventually I will find myself reacting to all situations which confront me as I was commanded in the scrolls to react, and soon these actions and reactions will become easy to perform, for any act with practice becomes easy.

Thus a new and good habit is born, for when an act becomes easy through constant repetition it becomes a pleasure to perform and if it is a pleasure to perform it is man's nature to perform it often. When I perform it often it becomes a habit and I become its slave and since it is a good habit this is my will.

Today I begin a new life.

And I make a solemn oath to myself that nothing will retard my new life's growth. I will lose not a day from these readings for that day cannot be retrieved nor can I substitute another for it. I must not,

I will not, break this habit of daily reading from these scrolls and, in truth, the few moments spent each day on this new habit are but a small price to pay for the happiness and success that will be mine.

As I read and re-read the words in the scrolls to follow, never will I allow the brevity of each scroll nor the simplicity of its words to cause me to treat the scroll's message lightly. Thousands of grapes are pressed to fill one jar with wine, and the grapeskin and pulp are tossed to the birds. So it is with these grapes of wisdom from the ages. Much has been filtered and tossed to the wind. Only the pure truth lies distilled in the words to come. I will drink as instructed and spill not a drop. And the seed of success I will swallow.

Today my old skin has become as dust. I will walk tall among men and they will know me not, for today I am a new man, with a new life.

CHAPTER NINE

The Scroll Marked II

I will greet this day with love in my heart.

For this is the greatest secret of success in all ventures. Muscle can split a shield and even destroy life but only the unseen power of love can open the hearts of men and until I master this art I will remain no more than a peddler in the market place. I will make love my greatest weapon and none on whom I call can defend against its force.

My reasoning they may counter; my speech they may distrust; my apparel they may disapprove; my face they may reject; and even my bargains may cause them suspicion; yet my love will melt all hearts liken to the sun whose rays soften the coldest clay.

I will greet this day with love in my heart.

And how will I do this? Henceforth will I look on all things with love and I will be born again. I will love the sun for it warms my bones; yet I will love the rain for it cleanses my spirit. I will love the light for it shows me the way; yet I will love the darkness for it shows me the stars. I will welcome happiness for it enlarges my heart; yet I will endure sadness for it opens my soul. I will acknowledge rewards for they are my due; yet I will welcome obstacles for they are my challenge.

I will greet this day with love in my heart.

And how will I speak? I will laud mine enemies and they will become friends; I will encourage my friends and they will become brothers. Always will I dig for reasons to applaud; never will I scratch for excuses to gossip. When I am tempted to criticize I will bite on my tongue; when I am moved to praise I will shout from the roofs.

Is it not so that birds, the wind, the sea and all nature speaks with the music of praise for their creator? Cannot I speak with the same music to his children? Henceforth will I remember this secret and it will change my life.

I will greet this day with love in my heart.

And how will I act? I will love all manners of men for each has qualities to be admired even though they be hidden. With love I will tear down the wall of suspicion and hate which they have built round their hearts and in its place will I build bridges so that my love may enter their souls.

I will love the ambitious for they can inspire me!

I will love the failures for they can teach me. I will love the kings for they are but human; I will love the meek for they are divine. I will love the rich for they are yet lonely; I will love the poor for they are so many. I will love the young for the faith they hold; I will love the old for the wisdom they share. I will love the beautiful for their eyes of sadness; I will love the ugly for their souls of peace.

I will greet this day with love in my heart.

But how will I react to the actions of others? With love. For just as love is my weapon to open the hearts of men, love is also my shield to repulse the arrows of hate and the spears of anger. Adversity and discouragement will beat against my new shield and become as the softest of rains. My shield will protect me in the market place and sustain me when I am alone. It will uplift me in moments of despair yet it will calm me in time of exultation. It will become stronger and more protective with use until one day I will cast it aside and walk unencumbered among all manners of men and, when I do, my name will be raised high on the pyramid of life.

I will greet this day with love in my heart.

And how will I confront each whom I meet? In only one way. In silence and to myself I will address him and say I Love You. Though spoken in silence these words will shine in my eyes, unwrinkle my brow, bring a smile to my lips, and echo in my voice; and his heart will be opened. And who is there who will say nay to my goods when his heart feels my love?

I will greet this day with love in my heart.

And most of all I will love myself. For when I do I will zealously inspect all things which enter my body, my mind, my soul, and my heart. Never will I overindulge the requests of my flesh, rather I will cherish my body with cleanliness and moderation. Never will I allow my mind to be attracted to evil and despair, rather I will uplift it with the knowledge and wisdom of the ages. Never will I allow my soul to become complacent and satisfied, rather I will feed it with meditation and prayer. Never will I allow my heart to become small and bitter, rather I will share it and it will grow and warm the earth.

I will greet this day with love in my heart.

Henceforth will I love all mankind. From this moment all hate is let from my veins for I have not time to hate, only time to love. From this moment I take the first step required to become a man among men. With love I will increase my sales a hundredfold and become a great salesman. If I have no other qualities I can succeed with love alone. Without it I will fail though I possess all the knowledge and skills of the world.

I will greet this day with love, and I will succeed.

CHAPTER TEN

The Scroll Marked III

I will persist until I succeed.

In the Orient young bulls are tested for the fight arena in a certain manner. Each is brought to the ring and allowed to attack a picador who pricks them with a lance. The bravery of each bull is then rated with care according to the number of times he demonstrates his willingness to charge in spite of the sting of the blade. Henceforth will I recognize that each day I am tested by life in like manner. If I persist, if I continue to try, if I continue to charge forward, I will succeed.

I will persist until I succeed.

I was not delivered unto this world in defeat, nor does failure course in my veins. I am not a sheep waiting to be prodded by my shepherd. I am a lion and I refuse to talk, to walk, to sleep with the sheep. I will hear not those who weep and complain, for their disease is contagious. Let them join the sheep. The slaughterhouse of failure is not my destiny.

I will persist until I succeed.

The prizes of life are at the end of each journey, not near the beginning; and it is not given to me to know how many steps are necessary in order to reach my goal. Failure I may still encounter at the thousandth step, yet success hides behind the next bend in the road. Never will I know how close it lies unless I turn the corner.

Always will I take another step. If that is of no avail I will take another, and yet another. In truth, one step at a time is not too difficult.

I will persist until I succeed.

Henceforth, I will consider each day's effort as but one blow of my blade against a mighty oak. The first blow may cause not a tremor in the wood, nor the second, nor the third. Each blow, of itself, may be trifling, and seem of no consequence. Yet from childish swipes the oak will eventually tumble. So it will be with my efforts of today.

I will be liken to the rain drop which washes away the mountain; the ant who devours a tiger; the star which brightens the earth; the slave who builds a pyramid. I will build my castle one brick at a time for I know that small attempts, repeated, will complete any undertaking.

I will persist until I succeed.

I will never consider defeat and I will remove from my vocabulary such words and phrases as quit, cannot, unable, impossible, out of the question, improbable, failure, unworkable, hopeless, and retreat; for they are the words of fools. I will avoid despair but if this disease of the mind should infect me then I will work on in despair. I will toil and I will endure. I will ignore the obstacles at my feet and keep mine eyes on the goals above my head, for I know that where dry desert ends, green grass grows.

I will persist until I succeed.

I will remember the ancient law of averages and I will bend it to my good. I will persist with knowledge that each failure to sell will increase my chance for success at the next attempt. Each nay I hear will bring me closer to the sound of yea. Each frown I meet only prepares me for the smile to come. Each misfortune I encounter will carry in it the seed of tomorrow's good luck. I must have the night to appreciate the day. I must fail often to succeed only once.

I will persist until I succeed.

. I will try, and try, and try again. Each obstacle I will consider as a mere detour to my goal and a challenge to my profession. I will persist and develop my skills as the mariner develops his, by learning to ride out the wrath of each storm.

I will persist until I succeed.

Henceforth, I will learn and apply another secret of those who excel in my work. When each day is ended, not regarding whether it has been a success or a failure, I will attempt to achieve one more sale. When my thoughts beckon my tired body homeward I will resist the temptation to depart. I will try again. I will make one more attempt to close with victory, and if that fails I will make another. Never will I allow any day to end with a failure. Thus will I plant the seed of tomorrow's success and gain an insurmountable advantage over those who cease their labor at a prescribed time. When others cease their struggle, then mine will begin, and my harvest will be full.

I will persist until I succeed.

Nor will I allow yesterday's success to lull me into today's complacency, for this is the great foundation of failure. I will forget the happenings of the day that is gone, whether they were good or bad, and greet the new sun with confidence that this will be the best day of my life.

So long as there is breath in me, that long will I persist. For now I know one of the greatest principles of success; if I persist long enough I will win.

I will persist.

I will win.

CHAPTER ELEVEN

The Scroll Marked IV

I am nature's greatest miracle.

Since the beginning of time never has there been another with my mind, my heart, my eyes, my ears, my hands, my hair, my mouth. None that came before, none that live today, and none that come tomorrow can walk and talk and move and think exactly like me. All men are my brothers yet I am different from each. I am a unique creature.

I am nature's greatest miracle.

Although I am of the animal kingdom, animal rewards alone will not satisfy me. Within me burns a flame which has been passed from generations uncounted and its heat is a constant irritation to my spirit to become better than I am, and I will. I will fan this flame of dissatisfaction and proclaim my uniqueness to the world.

None can duplicate my brush strokes, none can make my chisel marks, none can duplicate my handwriting, none can produce my child, and, in truth, none has the ability to sell exactly as I. Henceforth, I will capitalize on this difference for it is an asset to be promoted to the fullest.

I am nature's greatest miracle.

Vain attempts to imitate others no longer will I make. Instead will I place my uniqueness on display in the market place. I will proclaim it, yea, I will sell it. I will begin now to accent my differences; hide my similarities. So too will I apply this principle to the goods I sell. Salesman and goods, different from all others, and proud of the difference.

I am a unique creature of nature.

I am rare, and there is value in all rarity; therefore, I am valuable. I am the end product of thousands of years of evolution; therefore, I am better equipped in both mind and body than all the emperors and wise men who preceded me.

But my skills, my mind, my heart, and my body will stagnate, rot, and die lest I put them to good use. I have unlimited potential. Only a small portion of my brain do I employ; only a paltry amount of my muscles do I flex. A hundredfold or more can I increase my accomplishments of yesterday and this I will do, beginning today.

Nevermore will I be satisfied with yesterday's accomplishments nor will I indulge, anymore, in self-praise for deeds which in reality are too small to even acknowledge. I can accomplish far more than I have, and I will, for why should the miracle which produced me end with my birth? Why can I not extend that miracle to my deeds of today?

I am nature's greatest miracle.

I am not on this earth by chance. I am here for a purpose and that purpose is to grow into a mountain, not to shrink to a grain of sand. Henceforth will I apply all my efforts to become the highest mountain of all and I will strain my potential until it cries for mercy.

I will increase my knowledge of mankind, myself, and the goods I sell, thus my sales will multiply. I will practice, and improve, and polish the words I utter to sell my goods, for this is the foundation on which I will build my career and never will I forget that many have attained great wealth and success with only one sales talk, delivered with excellence. Also will I seek constantly to improve my manners and graces, for they are the sugar to which all are attracted.

I am nature's greatest miracle.

I will concentrate my energy on the challenge of the moment and my actions will help me forget all else. The problems of my home will be left in my home. I will think naught of my family when I am in the market place for this will cloud my thoughts. So too will the problems of the market place be left in the market place and I will think naught of my profession when I am in my home for this will dampen my love.

There is no room in the market place for my

family, nor is there room in my home for the market. Each I will divorce from the other and thus will I remain wedded to both. Separate must they remain or my career will die. This is a paradox of the ages.

I am nature's greatest miracle.

I have been given eyes to see and a mind to think and now I know a great secret of life for I perceive, at last, that all my problems, discouragements, and heartaches are, in truth, great opportunities in disguise. I will no longer be fooled by the garments they wear for mine eyes are open. I will look beyond the cloth and I will not be deceived.

I am nature's greatest miracle.

No beast, no plant, no wind, no rain, no rock, no lake had the same beginning as I, for I was conceived in love and brought forth with a purpose. In the past I have not considered this fact but it will henceforth shape and guide my life.

I am nature's greatest miracle.

And nature knows not defeat. Eventually, she emerges victorious and so will I, and with each victory the next struggle becomes less difficult.

I will win, and I will become a great salesman, for I am unique.

I am nature's greatest miracle.

CHAPTER TWELVE

The Scroll Marked V

I will live this day as if it is my last.

And what shall I do with this last precious day which remains in my keeping? First, I will seal up its container of life so that not one drop spills itself upon the sand. I will waste not a moment mourning yesterday's misfortunes, yesterday's defeats, yesterday's aches of the heart, for why should I throw good after bad?

Can sand flow upward in the hour glass? Will the sun rise where it sets and set where it rises? Can I relive the errors of yesterday and right them? Can I call back yesterday's wounds and make them whole? Can I become younger than yesterday? Can I take back the evil that was spoken, the blows that were struck, the pain that was caused? No. Yesterday is buried forever and I will think of it no more.

I will live this day as if it is my last.

And what then shall I do? Forgetting yesterday neither will I think of tomorrow. Why should I throw *now* after *maybe*? Can tomorrow's sand flow through the glass before today's? Will the sun rise twice this morning? Can I perform tomorrow's deeds while standing in today's path? Can I place tomorrow's gold in today's purse? Can tomorrow's child be born today? Can tomorrow's death cast its shadow backward and darken today's joy? Should I concern myself over events which I may never witness? Should I torment myself with problems that may never come to pass? No! Tomorrow lies buried with yesterday, and I will think of it no more.

I will live this day as if it is my last.

This day is all I have and these hours are now my eternity. I greet this sunrise with cries of joy as a prisoner who is reprieved from death. I lift mine arms with thanks for this priceless gift of a new day. So too, I will beat upon my heart with gratitude as I consider all who greeted yesterday's sunrise who are no longer with the living today. I am indeed a fortunate man and today's hours are but a bonus, undeserved. Why have I been allowed to live this extra day when others, far better than I, have departed? Is it that they have accomplished their purpose while mine is yet to be achieved? Is this another opportunity for me to become the man I know I can be? Is there a purpose in nature? Is this my day to excel?

I will live this day as if it is my last.

I have but one life and life is naught but a measurement of time. When I waste one I destroy the other. If I waste today I destroy the last page of my life. Therefore, each hour of this day will I cherish for it can never return. It cannot be banked today to be withdrawn on the morrow, for who can trap the wind? Each minute of this day will I grasp with both hands and fondle with love for its value is beyond price. What dying man can purchase another breath though he willingly give all his gold? What price dare I place on the hours ahead? I will make them priceless!

I will live this day as if it is my last.

I will avoid with fury the killers of time. Procrastination I will destroy with action; doubt I will bury under faith; fear I will dismember with confidence. Where there are idle mouths I will listen not; where there are idle hands I will linger not; where there are idle bodies I will visit not. Henceforth I know that to court idleness is to steal food, clothing, and warmth from those I love. I am not a thief. I am a man of love and today is my last chance to prove my love and my greatness.

I will live this day as if it is my last.

The duties of today I shall fulfill today. Today I shall fondle my children while they are young; tomorrow they will be gone, and so will I. Today I shall embrace my woman with sweet kisses; tomorrow she will be gone, and so will I. Today I shall lift up a friend in need; tomorrow he will no longer cry for help, nor will I hear his cries. Today I shall give myself in sacrifice and work; tomorrow I will have nothing to give, and there will be none to receive.

I will live this day as if it is my last.

And if it is my last, it will be my greatest monument. This day I will make the best day of my life. This day I will drink every minute to its full. I will savor its taste and give thanks. I will maketh every hour count and each minute I will trade only for something of value. I will labor harder than ever before and push my muscles until they cry for relief, and then I will continue. I will make more calls than ever before. I will sell more goods than ever before. I will earn more gold than ever before. Each minute of today will be more fruitful than hours of yesterday. My last must be my best.

I will live this day as if it is my last.

And if it is not, I shall fall to my knees and give thanks.

CHAPTER
THIRTEEN

The Scroll Marked VI

Today I will be master of my emotions.

The tides advance; the tides recede. Winter goes and summer comes. Summer wanes and the cold increases. The sun rises; the sun sets. The moon is full; the moon is black. The birds arrive; the birds depart. Flowers bloom; flowers fade. Seeds are sown; harvests are reaped. All nature is a circle of moods and I am a part of nature and so, like the tides, my moods will rise; my moods will fall.

Today I will be master of my emotions.

It is one of nature's tricks, little understood, that each day I awaken with moods that have changed from yesterday. Yesterday's joy will become today's sadness; yet today's sadness will grow into tomorrow's joy. Inside me is a wheel, constantly turning from sadness to joy, from exultation to depression, from happiness to melancholy. Like the flowers, today's full bloom of joy will fade and wither into despondency, yet I will remember that as today's dead flower carries the seed of tomorrow's bloom so, too, does today's sadness carry the seed of tomorrow's joy.

Today I will be master of my emotions.

And how will I master these emotions so that each day will be productive? For unless my mood is right the day will be a failure. Trees and plants depend on the weather to flourish but I make my own weather, yea I transport it with me. If I bring rain and gloom and darkness and pessimism to my customers then they will react with rain and gloom and darkness and pessimism and they will purchase naught. If I bring joy and enthusiasm and brightness and laughter to my customers they will react with joy and enthusiasm and brightness and laughter and my weather will produce a harvest of sales and a granary of gold for me.

Today I will be master of my emotions.

And how will I master my emotions so that every day is a happy day, and a productive one? I will learn this secret of the ages: *Weak is he who permits his thoughts to control his actions; strong is he who forces his actions to control his thoughts.* Each day, when I awaken, I will follow this plan of battle before I am captured by the forces of sadness, self-pity and failure—

If I feel depressed I will sing.
If I feel sad I will laugh.
If I feel ill I will double my labor.
If I feel fear I will plunge ahead.
If I feel inferior I will wear new garments.
If I feel uncertain I will raise my voice.
If I feel poverty I will think of wealth to come.
If I feel incompetent I will remember past success.
If I feel insignificant I will remember my goals.
Today I will be master of my emotions.

Henceforth, I will know that only those with inferior ability can always be at their best, and I am not inferior. There will be days when I must constantly struggle against forces which would tear me down. Those such as despair and sadness are simple to recognize but there are others which approach with a smile and the hand of friendship and they can also destroy me. Against them, too, I must never relinquish control—

If I become overconfident I will recall my failures.
If I overindulge I will think of past hungers.
If I feel complacency I will remember my competition.
If I enjoy moments of greatness I will remember moments of shame.
If I feel all-powerful I will try to stop the wind.
If I attain great wealth I will remember one unfed mouth.
If I become overly proud I will remember a moment of weakness.

If I feel my skill is unmatched I will look at the stars.

Today I will be master of my emotions.

And with this new knowledge I will also understand and recognize the moods of he on whom I call. I will make allowances for his anger and irritation of today for he knows not the secret of controlling his mind. I can withstand his arrows and insults for now I know that tomorrow he will change and be a joy to approach.

No longer will I judge a man on one meeting; no longer will I fail to call again tomorrow on he who meets me with hate today. This day he will not buy gold chariots for a penny, yet tomorrow he would exchange his home for a tree. My knowledge of this secret will be my key to great wealth.

Today I will be master of my emotions.

Henceforth I will recognize and identify the mystery of moods in all mankind, and in me. From this moment I am prepared to control whatever personality awakes in me each day. I will master my moods through positive action and when I master my moods I will control my destiny.

Today I control my destiny, and my destiny is to become the greatest salesman in the world!

I will become master of myself.

I will become great.

CHAPTER FOURTEEN

The Scroll Marked VII

I will laugh at the world.

No living creature can laugh except man. Trees may bleed when they are wounded, and beasts in the field will cry in pain and hunger, yet only I have the gift of laughter and it is mine to use whenever I choose. Henceforth I will cultivate the habit of laughter.

I will smile and my digestion will improve; I will chuckle and my burdens will be lightened; I will laugh and my life will be lengthened for this is the great secret of long life and now it is mine.

I will laugh at the world.

And most of all, I will laugh at myself for man is most comical when he takes himself too seriously. Never will I fall into this trap of the mind. For though I be nature's greatest miracle am I not still a mere grain tossed about by the winds of time? Do I truly know whence I came or whither I am bound? Will my concern for this day not seem foolish ten years hence? Why should I permit the petty happenings of today to disturb me? What can take place before this sun sets which will not seem insignificant in the river of centuries?

I will laugh at the world.

And how can I laugh when confronted with man or deed which offends me so as to bring forth my tears or my curses? Four words I will train myself to. say until they become a habit so strong that immediately they will appear in my mind whenever good humor threatens to depart from me. These words, passed down from the ancients, will carry me through every adversity and maintain my life in balance. These four words are: *This too shall pass.*

I will laugh at the world.

For all worldly things shall indeed pass. When I am heavy with heartache I shall console myself that this too shall pass; when I am puffed with success I shall warn myself that this too shall pass. When I am strangled in poverty I shall tell myself that this too shall pass; when I am burdened with wealth I shall tell myself that this too shall pass. Yea, verily, where is he who built the pyramid? Is he not buried within its stone? And will the pyramid, one day, not also be buried under sand? If all things shall pass why should I be of concern for today?

I will laugh at the world.

I will paint this day with laughter; I will frame

this night in song. Never will I labor to be happy; rather will I remain too busy to be sad. I will enjoy today's happiness today. It is not grain to be stored in a box. It is not wine to be saved in a jar. It cannot be saved for the morrow. It must be sown and reaped on the same day and this I will do, henceforth.

I will laugh at the world.

And with my laughter all things will be reduced to their proper size. I will laugh at my failures and they will vanish in clouds of new dreams; I will laugh at my successes and they will shrink to their true value. I will laugh at evil and it will die untasted; I will laugh at goodness and it will thrive and abound. Each day will be triumphant only when my smiles bring forth smiles from others and this I do in selfishness, for those on whom I frown are those who purchase not my goods.

I will laugh at the world.

Henceforth will I shed only tears of sweat, for those of sadness or remorse or frustration are of no value in the market place whilst each smile can be exchanged for gold and each kind word, spoken from my heart, can build a castle.

Never will I allow myself to become so important, so wise, so dignified, so powerful, that I forget how to laugh at myself and my world. In this matter I will always remain as a child, for only as a child am I given the ability to look up to others; and so long as I look up to another I will never grow too long for my cot.

I will laugh at the world.

And so long as I can laugh never will I be poor.

─────────────

This, then, is one of nature's greatest gifts, and I will waste it no more. Only with laughter and happiness can I truly become a success. Only with laughter and happiness can I enjoy the fruits of my labor. Were it not so, far better would it be to fail, for happiness is the wine that sharpens the taste of the meal. To enjoy success I must have happiness, and laughter will be the maiden who serves me.

I will be happy.

I will be successful.

I will be the greatest salesman the world has ever known.

CHAPTER
FIFTEEN

The Scroll Marked VIII

Today I will multiply my value a hundredfold.

A mulberry leaf touched with the genius of man becomes silk.

A field of clay touched with the genius of man becomes a castle.

A cyprus tree touched with the genius of man becomes a shrine.

A cut of sheep's hair touched with the genius of man becomes raiment for a king.

If it is possible for leaves and clay and wood and hair to have their value multiplied a hundred, yea a thousandfold by man, cannot I do the same with the clay which bears my name?

Today I will multiply my value a hundredfold.

I am liken to a grain of wheat which faces one of three futures. The wheat can be placed in a sack and dumped in a stall until it is fed to swine. Or it can be ground to flour and made into bread. Or it can be placed in the earth and allowed to grow until its golden head divides and produces a thousand grains from the one.

I am liken to a grain of wheat with one difference. The wheat cannot choose whether it be fed to swine, ground for bread, or planted to multiply. I have a choice and I will not let my life be fed to swine nor will I let it be ground under the rocks of failure and despair to be broken open and devoured by the will of others.

Today I will multiply my value a hundredfold.

To grow and multiply it is necessary to plant the wheat grain in the darkness of the earth and my failures, my despairs, my ignorance, and my inabilities are the darkness in which I have been planted in order to ripen. Now, like the wheat grain which will sprout and blossom only if it is nurtured with rain and sun and warm winds, I too must nurture my body and mind to fulfill my dreams. But to grow to full stature the wheat must wait on the whims of nature. I need not wait for I have the power to choose my own destiny.

Today I will multiply my value a hundredfold.

And how will I accomplish this? First I will set goals for the day, the week, the month, the year, and my life. Just as the rain must fall before the wheat will crack its shell and sprout, so must I have objectives before my life will crystallize. In setting my goals I will consider my best performance of the past and multiply it a hundredfold. This will be the standard by which I will live in the future. Never will I be of concern that my goals are too high for is it not better to aim my spear at the moon and strike only an eagle than to aim my spear at the eagle and strike only a rock?

Today I will multiply my value a hundredfold.

The height of my goals will not hold me in awe though I may stumble often before they are reached. If I stumble I will rise and my falls will not concern me for all men must stumble often to reach the hearth. Only a worm is free from the worry of stumbling. I am not a worm. I am not an onion plant. I am not a sheep. I am a man. Let others build a cave with their clay. I will build a castle with mine.

Today I will multiply my value a hundredfold.

And just as the sun must warm the earth to bring forth the seedling of wheat so, too, will the words on these scrolls warm my life and turn my dreams into reality. Today I will surpass every action which I performed yesterday. I will climb today's mountain to the utmost of my ability yet tomorrow I will climb higher than today, and the next will be higher than tomorrow. To surpass the deeds of others is unimportant; to surpass my own deeds is all.

Today I will multiply my value a hundredfold.

And just as the warm wind guides the wheat to maturity, the same winds will carry my voice to those who will listen and my words will announce my goals. Once spoken I dare not recall them lest I lose face. I will be as my own prophet and though all may laugh at my utterances they will hear my plans, they will know my dreams; and thus there will be no escape for me until my words become accomplished deeds.

Today I will multiply my value a hundredfold.

I will commit not the terrible crime of aiming too low.

I will do the work that a failure will not do.

I will always let my reach exceed my grasp.

I will never be content with my performance in the market.

I will always raise my goals as soon as they are attained.

I will always strive to make the next hour better than this one.

I will always announce my goals to the world.

Yet, never will I proclaim my accomplishments. Let the world, instead, approach me with praise and may I have the wisdom to receive it in humility.

Today I will multiply my value a hundredfold.

One grain of wheat when multiplied a hundredfold will produce a hundred stalks. Multiply these a hundredfold, ten times, and they will feed all the cities of the earth. Am I not more than a grain of wheat?

Today I will multiply my value a hundredfold.

And when it is done I will do it again, and again, and there will be astonishment and wonder at my greatness as the words of these scrolls are fulfilled in me.

CHAPTER
SIXTEEN

The Scroll Marked IX

My dreams are worthless, my plans are dust, my goals are impossible.

All are of no value unless they are followed by action.

I will act now.

Never has there been a map, however carefully executed to detail and scale, which carried its owner over even one inch of ground. Never has there been a parchment of law, however fair, which prevented one crime. Never has there been a scroll, even such as the one I hold, which earned so much as a penny or produced a single word of acclamation. Action, alone, is the tinder which ignites the map, the parchment, this scroll, my dreams, my plans, my goals, into a living force. Action is the food and drink which will nourish my success.

I will act now.

My procrastination which has held me back was born of fear and now I recognize this secret mined from the depths of all courageous hearts. Now I know that to conquer fear I must always act without hesitation and the flutters in my heart will vanish. Now I know that action reduces the lion of terror to an ant of equanimity.

I will act now.

Henceforth, I will remember the lesson of the firefly who gives of its light only when it is on the wing, only when it is in action. I will become a firefly and even in the day my glow will be seen in spite of the sun. Let others be as butterflies who preen their wings yet depend on the charity of a flower for life. I will be as the firefly and my light will brighten the world.

I will act now.

I will not avoid the tasks of today and charge them to tomorrow for I know that tomorrow never comes. Let me act now even though my actions may not bring happiness or success for it is better to act and fail than not to act and flounder. Happiness, in truth, may not be the fruit plucked by my action yet without action all fruit will die on the vine.

I will act now.

I will act now. I will act now. I will act now. Henceforth, I will repeat these words again and again and again, each hour, each day, every day, until the words become as much a habit as my breathing and the actions which follow become as instinctive as the blinking of my eyelids. With these words I can condition my mind to perform every act necessary for my success. With these words I can condition my mind to meet every challenge which the failure avoids.

I will act now.

I will repeat these words again and again and again.

When I awake I will say them and leap from my cot while the failure sleeps yet another hour.

I will act now.

When I enter the market place I will say them and immediately confront my first prospect while the failure ponders yet his possibility of rebuff.

I will act now.

When I face a closed door I will say them and knock while the failure waits outside with fear and trepidation.

I will act now.

When I face temptation I will say them and immediately act to remove myself from evil.

I will act now.

When I am tempted to quit and begin again tomorrow I will say them and immediately act to consummate another sale.

I will act now.

Only action determines my value in the market place and to multiply my value I will multiply my actions. I will walk where the failure fears to walk. I will work when the failure seeks rest. I will talk when the failure remains silent. I will call on ten who can buy my goods while the failure makes grand plans to call on one. I will say it is done before the failure says it is too late.

I will act now.

For now is all I have. Tomorrow is the day reserved for the labor of the lazy. I am not lazy. Tomorrow is the day when the evil become good. I am not evil. Tomorrow is the day when the weak become strong. I am not weak. Tomorrow is the day when the failure will succeed. I am not a failure.

I will act now.

When the lion is hungry he eats. When the eagle has thirst he drinks. Lest they act, both will perish.

I hunger for success. I thirst for happiness and peace of mind. Lest I act I will perish in a life of failure, misery, and sleepless nights.

I will command, and I will obey mine own command.

I will act now.

Success will not wait. If I delay she will become betrothed to another and lost to me forever.

This is the time. This is the place. I am the man.

I will act now.

CHAPTER SEVENTEEN

The Scroll Marked X

Who is of so little faith that in a moment of great disaster or heartbreak has not called to his God? Who has not cried out when confronted with danger, death, or mystery beyond his normal experience or comprehension? From where has this deep instinct come which escapes from the mouth of all living creatures in moments of peril?

Move your hand in haste before another's eyes and his eyelids will blink. Tap another on his knee and his leg will jump. Confront another with dark horror and his mouth will say, "My God" from the same deep impulse.

My life need not be filled with religion in order for me to recognize this greatest mystery of nature. All creatures that walk the earth, including man, possess the instinct to cry for help. Why do we possess this instinct, this gift?

Are not our cries a form of prayer? Is it not incomprehensible in a world governed by nature's laws to give a lamb, or a mule, or a bird, or man the instinct to cry out for help lest some great mind has also provided that the cry should be heard by some superior power having the ability to hear and to answer our cry? Henceforth I will pray, but my cries for help will only be cries for guidance.

Never will I pray for the material things of the world. I am not calling to a servant to bring me food. I am not ordering an innkeeper to provide me with room. Never will I seek delivery of gold, love, good health, petty victories, fame, success, or happiness. Only for guidance will I pray, that I may be shown the way to acquire these things, and my prayer will always be answered.

The guidance I seek may come, or the guidance I seek may not come, but are not both of these an answer? If a child seeks bread from his father and it is not forthcoming has not the father answered?

I will pray for guidance, and I will pray as a salesman, in this manner—

O creator of all things, help me. For this day I go out into the world naked and alone, and without your hand to guide me I will wander far from the path which leads to success and happiness.

*　　*　　*

I ask not for gold or garments or even opportunities equal to my ability; instead, guide me so that I may acquire ability equal to my opportunities.

You have taught the lion and the eagle how to hunt and prosper with teeth and claw. Teach me how to hunt with words and prosper with love so that I may be a lion among men and an eagle in the market place.

Help me to remain humble through obstacles and failures; yet hide not from mine eyes the prize that will come with victory.

Assign me tasks to which others have failed; yet guide me to pluck the seeds of success from their failures. Confront me with fears that will temper my spirit; yet endow me with courage to laugh at my misgivings.

Spare me sufficient days to reach my goals; yet help me to live this day as though it be my last.

Guide me in my words that they may bear fruit; yet silence me from gossip that none be maligned.

Discipline me in the habit of trying and trying again; yet show me the way to make use of the law of averages. Favor me with alertness to recognize opportunity; yet endow me with patience which will concentrate my strength.

Bathe me in good habits that the bad ones may drown; yet grant me compassion for weaknesses in others. Suffer me to know that all things shall pass; yet help me to count my blessings of today.

Expose me to hate so it not be a stranger; yet fill my cup with love to turn strangers into friends.

But all these things be only if thy will. I am a small and a lonely grape clutching the vine yet thou hast made me different from all others. Verily, there must be a special place for me. Guide me. Help me. Show me the way.

Let me become all you planned for me when my seed was planted and selected by you to sprout in the vineyard of the world.

Help this humble salesman.
Guide me, God.

CHAPTER EIGHTEEN

And so it came to pass that Hafid waited in his lonely palace for he who was to receive the scrolls. The old man, with only his trusted bookkeeper for a companion, watched the seasons come and go, and the infirmities of old age soon prevented him from doing little except sit quietly in his covered garden.

He waited.

He waited nearly three full years after the disposal of his worldly wealth and the disbanding of his trade empire.

And then from out of the desert to the East there appeared a slight, limping figure of a stranger who entered Damascus and made straightway through the streets until he stood before the palace of Hafid. Erasmus, usually a model of courtesy and propriety, remained resolutely in the doorway as the caller repeated his request, "I wouldst speak with thy master."

The stranger's appearance was not one to inspire confidence. His sandals were ripped and mended with rope, his brown legs were cut and scratched and had sores in many places, and above them hung a loose and tattered camel's hair loincloth. The man's hair was snarled and long and his eyes, red from the sun, seemed to burn from within.

Erasmus held tightly to the door handle. "What is it thou seeketh of my sire?"

The stranger allowed his sack to fall from his shoulders and clenched both hands in prayer toward Erasmus. "Please, kind man, grant me an audience with thy master. I mean him no harm nor seek I alms. Let him hear my words and then I will go in haste if I offend him."

Erasmus, still unsure, slowly opened the door and nodded toward the interior. Then he turned without looking back and walked swiftly toward the garden with his visitor limping behind.

In the garden, Hafid dozed, and Erasmus hesitated before his master. He coughed and Hafid stirred. He coughed again and the old man opened his eyes.

"Forgive this disturbance, master, but there is a caller."

Hafid, now awake, sat up and shifted his gaze to the stranger who bowed and spoke. "Art thou he who has been called the greatest salesman in the world?"

Hafid frowned but nodded, "I have been called

that in years now gone. No longer is that crown on my old head. What seeketh thee of me?"

The small visitor stood self-consciously before Hafid and rubbed his hands over his matted chest. He blinked his eyes in the soft light and replied, "I am called Saul and I return now, from Jerusalem, to my birthplace in Tarsus. However, I beg you, let not my appearance deceive you. I am not a bandit from the wilderness nor am I a beggar of the streets. I am a citizen of Tarsus and also a citizen of Rome. My people are Pharisees of the Jewish tribe of Benjamin and although I am a tentmaker by trade, I have studied under the great Gamaliel. Some call me Paul." He swayed as he spoke and Hafid, not fully awake until this moment, apologetically motioned for his visitor to sit.

Paul nodded but remained standing. "I come to thee for guidance and help which only you can give. Will you permit me, sire, to tell my story?"

Erasmus, standing behind the stranger, shook his head violently, but Hafid pretended not to notice. He studied the intruder of his sleep carefully and then nodded, "I am too old to continue to look up at thee. Sit at my feet and I will hear you through."

Paul pushed his sack aside and knelt near the old man who waited in silence.

"Four years ago, because the accumulated knowledge of too many years of study had blinded my heart to truth, I was the official witness to the stoning, in Jerusalem, of a holy man called Stephen. He had been condemned to death by the Jewish Sanhedrin for blasphemy against our God."

Hafid interrupted with puzzlement in his voice, "I do not understand how I am connected with this activity."

Paul raised his hand as if to calm the old man. "I will explain quickly. Stephen was a follower of a man called Jesus, who less than a year before the stoning of Stephen, was crucified by the Romans for sedition against the state. Stephen's guilt was his insistence that Jesus was the Messiah whose coming had been foretold by the Jewish prophets, and that the Temple had conspired with Rome to murder this son of God. This rebuke to those in authority could only be punishable with death and as I have already told thee, I participated.

"Furthermore, with my fanaticism and youthful zeal, I was supplied with letters from the high priest of the Temple and entrusted with the mission of journeying here to Damascus to search out every follower of Jesus and return them in chains to Jerusalem for punishment. This was, as I have said, four years ago."

Erasmus glanced at Hafid and was startled, for there was a look in the old man's eyes which had not been seen by the faithful bookkeeper in many years. Only the splash of fountain water could be heard in the garden until Paul spoke once more.

"Now as I approached Damascus with murder in my heart there was a sudden flash of light from the heavens. I remember not having been struck but I found myself on the ground and although I could not see, I could hear, and I heard a voice in my ear say, 'Saul, Saul, why do you persecute me?' I answered, 'Who are you?' and the voice replied, 'I am Jesus, whom you are persecuting; but rise and enter the city, and you will be told what to do.'

"I arose and was led by the hands of my companions into Damascus and there I was not able to eat or drink for three days while I remained in the house of a follower of the crucified one. Then I was visited by another called Ananias, who said he had been visited in a vision and told to come to me. Then he laid his hands upon my eyes and I could see again. Then I ate, and I drank, and my strength returned."

Hafid now leaned forward from his bench and inquired, "What then took place?"

"I was brought to the synagogue and my presence as a persecutor of the followers of Jesus struck fear into the hearts of all his followers but I preached nevertheless and my words confounded them, for now I spoke that he who had been crucified was indeed the Son of God.

"And all who listened suspected a trick of deceit on my part for had I not caused havoc in Jerusalem? I could not convince them of my change of heart and many plotted my death so I escaped over the walls and returned to Jerusalem.

"In Jerusalem the happenings of Damascus repeated themselves. None of the followers of Jesus would come near me although word had been received of my preaching in Damascus. Nevertheless, I continued to preach in the name of Jesus but it was of no avail. Everywhere I spoke I antagonized those who listened until one day I went to the Temple and in the courtyard, as I watched the sale of doves and lambs for sacrifice, the voice came to me again."

"This time what did it say?" Erasmus spoke before he could stop himself. Hafid smiled at his old friend and nodded for Paul to continue.

"The voice said, 'Thou hast had the Word for nearly four years but thou hast shown few the light. Even the word of God must be sold to the people or they will hear it not. Did not I speak in parables so that all might understand? Thou wilt catch few flies with vinegar. Return to Damascus and seek out he who is acclaimed as the greatest salesman in the world. If thou wouldst spread my word to the world let him show you the way.' "

Hafid glanced quickly at Erasmus and the old bookkeeper sensed the unspoken question. Was this the one for whom he had waited so long? The great salesman leaned forward and placed his hand on Paul's shoulder. "Tell me about this Jesus."

Paul, his voice now alive with new strength and volume, told of Jesus and his life. While the two listened, he spoke of the long Jewish wait for a Messiah who would come and unite them within a new and independent kingdom of happiness and peace. He told of John the Baptist and the arrival, on the stage of history, of one called Jesus. He told of the miracles performed by this man, his lectures to the crowds, his raising of the dead, his treatment of the money changers, and he told of the crucifixion, burial, and resurrection. Finally, as if to give further impact to his story, Paul reached into the sack at his side and removed a red garment which he placed in the lap of Hafid. "Sire, you hold in your arms all the worldly goods left behind by this Jesus. All that he possessed he shared with the world, even unto his life. And at the foot of his cross, Roman soldiers cast lots for this robe. It has come into my possession through much diligence and searching when I was last in Jerusalem."

Hafid's face paled and his hands shook as he turned the robe stained with blood. Erasmus, alarmed at his master's appearance, moved closer to the old man. Hafid continued to turn the garment until he found the small star sewn into the cloth . . . the mark of Tola, whose guild made the robes sold by Pathros. Next to the star was a circle sewn within a square . . . the mark of Pathros.

As Paul and Erasmus watched, the old man raised the robe and rubbed it gently against his cheek. Hafid shook his head. Impossible. Thousands of other robes were made by Tola and sold by Pathros in the years of his great trade route.

Still clutching the robe and speaking in a hoarse whisper, Hafid said, "Tell me what is known of the birth of this Jesus."

Paul said, "He left our world with little. He had entered it with less. He was born in a cave, in Bethlehem, during the time of the census of Tiberius."

Hafid's smile seemed almost childish to the two men, and they looked on with puzzlement, for tears also flowed down his wrinkled cheeks. He brushed them away with his hand and asked, "And was there not the brightest star that man has ever seen which shone above the birthplace of this baby?"

Paul's mouth opened yet he could not speak, nor was it necessary. Hafid raised his arms and embraced Paul, and this time the tears of both were mingled.

Finally the old man arose and beckoned toward Erasmus. "Faithful friend, go to the tower and return with the chest. We have found our salesman at last."

ABOUT THE AUTHOR

Og Mandino's books, with multi-million copy sales, make him the most widely read inspirational and self-help author in the world during the past decade.

In 1976, at the age of fifty-two, he shocked the publishing industry by resigning his presidency of SUCCESS UNLIMITED magazine to devote all his time to writing and lecturing and he is now one of the most sought-after speakers in the country.

Countless thousands in seventeen nations, from American corporate executives to Japanese factory workers, from Mexican prison convicts to Dutch housewives, from National Football League coaches to nuns in the Philippines, have acknowledged in their letters the great debt they owe Og Mandino for the miracle his words have wrought in their lives.